UNICORN
ACTIVITY BOOK FOR KIDS

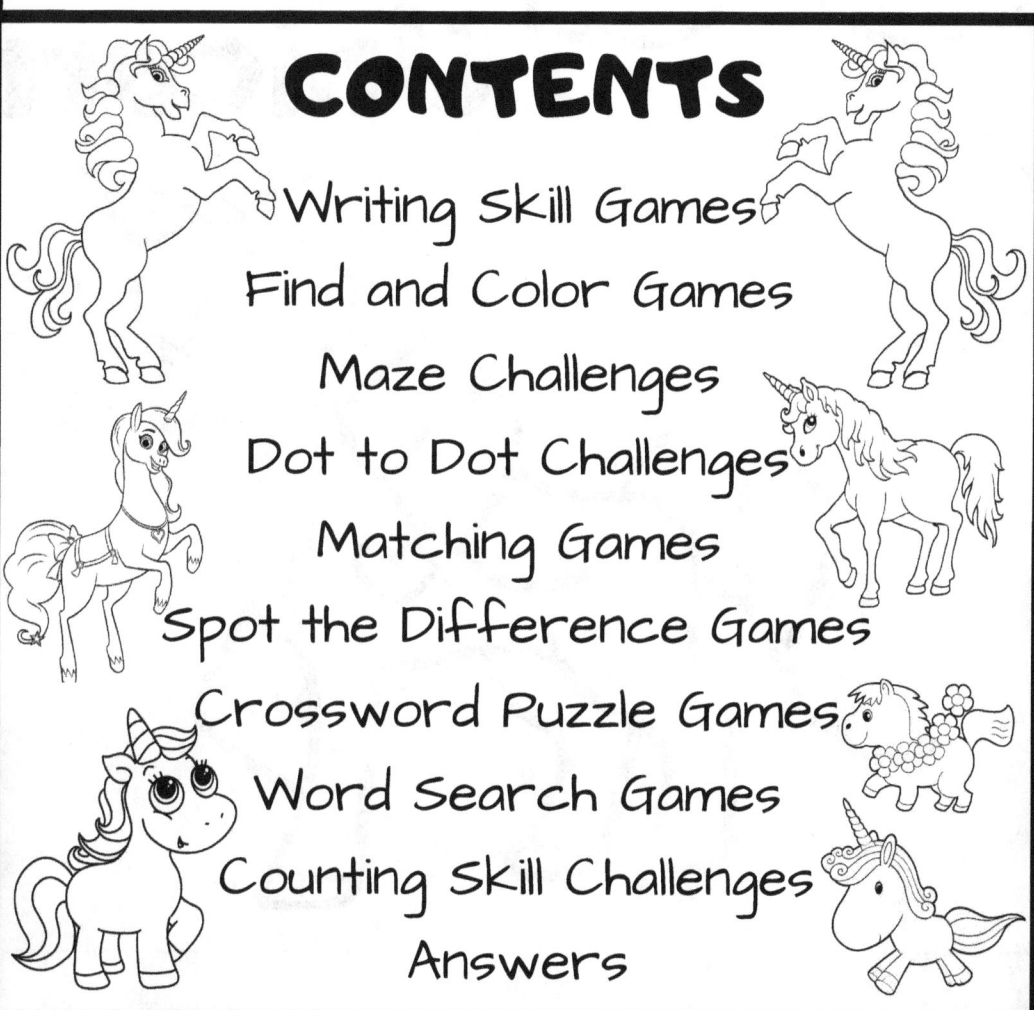

CONTENTS

Writing Skill Games

Find and Color Games

Maze Challenges

Dot to Dot Challenges

Matching Games

Spot the Difference Games

Crossword Puzzle Games

Word Search Games

Counting Skill Challenges

Answers

THIS COLORING BOOK BELONGS TO:

Writing Skill Game:

Uu is for
Unicorn

Find and Color Game:

Can you color the unicorn with their assigned color?

1 - pink	3 - red	5 - yellow
2 - violet	4 - orange	6 - blue

Maze Challenge:

Can you help the unicorn to find the way to the castle?

castle

Dot to dots challenge:
Can you connect the dots to create
a charming unicorn?

Matching Test:

Can you encircle the correct unicorn's shadow?

Spot the Difference Game:
Can you find and encircle the difference?

Crossword Puzzle Game:
Can you guess the hidden letters?

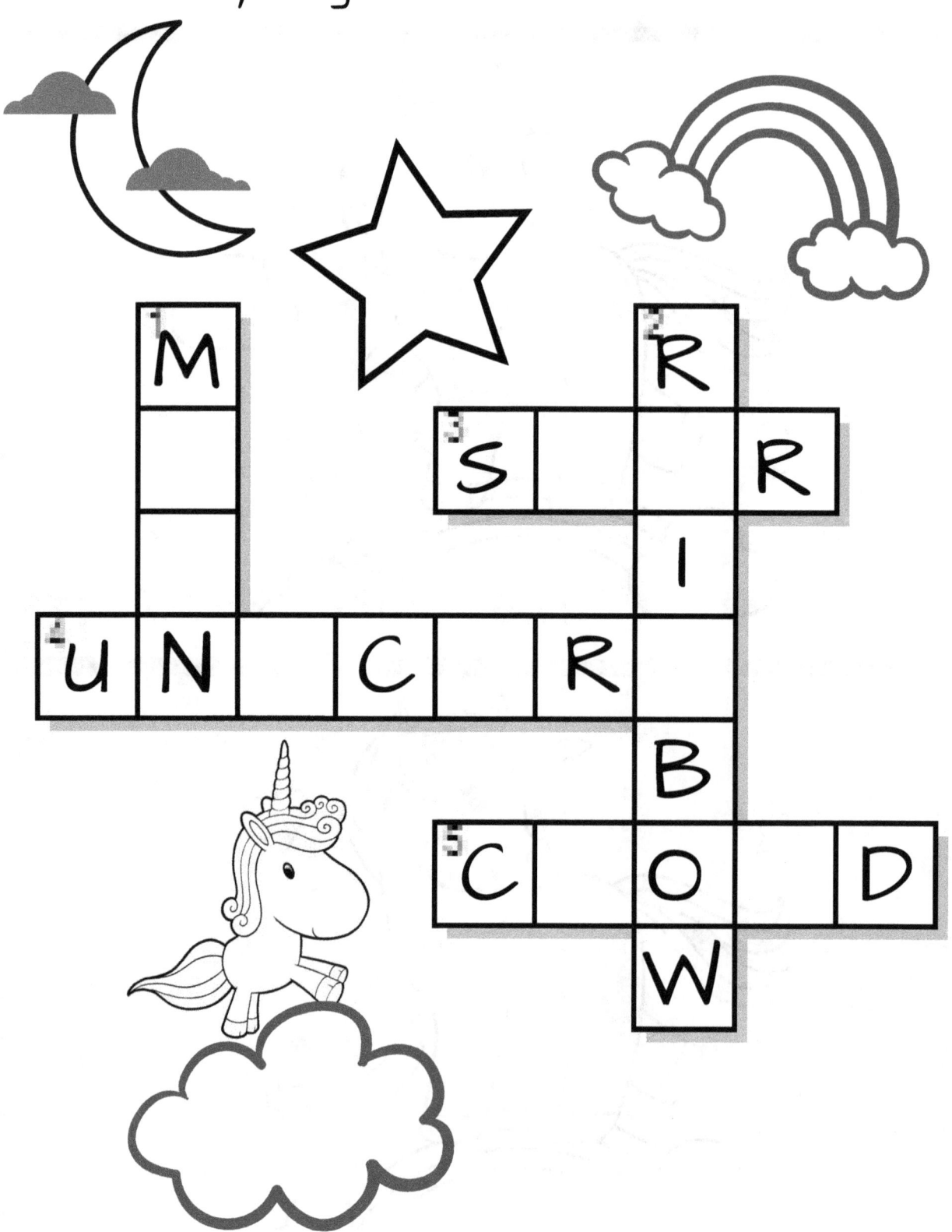

Word Search Challenge:

Can you find the 5 unicorn words?

```
U  L  F  L  P  D  U  U  D  J
N  U  T  D  O  H  N  N  Z  V
I  N  R  T  L  F  I  I  H  Z
C  I  K  B  N  G  C  C  I  U
O  C  E  V  R  O  O  O  E  K
R  O  G  L  T  Z  R  R  E  D
N  R  C  X  Z  A  N  N  H  E
U  N  I  C  O  R  N  G  F  N
M  C  I  L  Q  P  O  X  V  Q
P  Q  Q  X  O  W  V  P  N  E
```

UNICORN   UNICORN   UNICORN

UNICORN   UNICORN

Counting Skills Challenge:

Can you count how many unicorns?

Writing Skill Game: Can you draw the capital letter U?

Writing Skill Game: Can you draw the small letter U?

Writing Skill Game:

Can you help the unicorn to get the sweets?

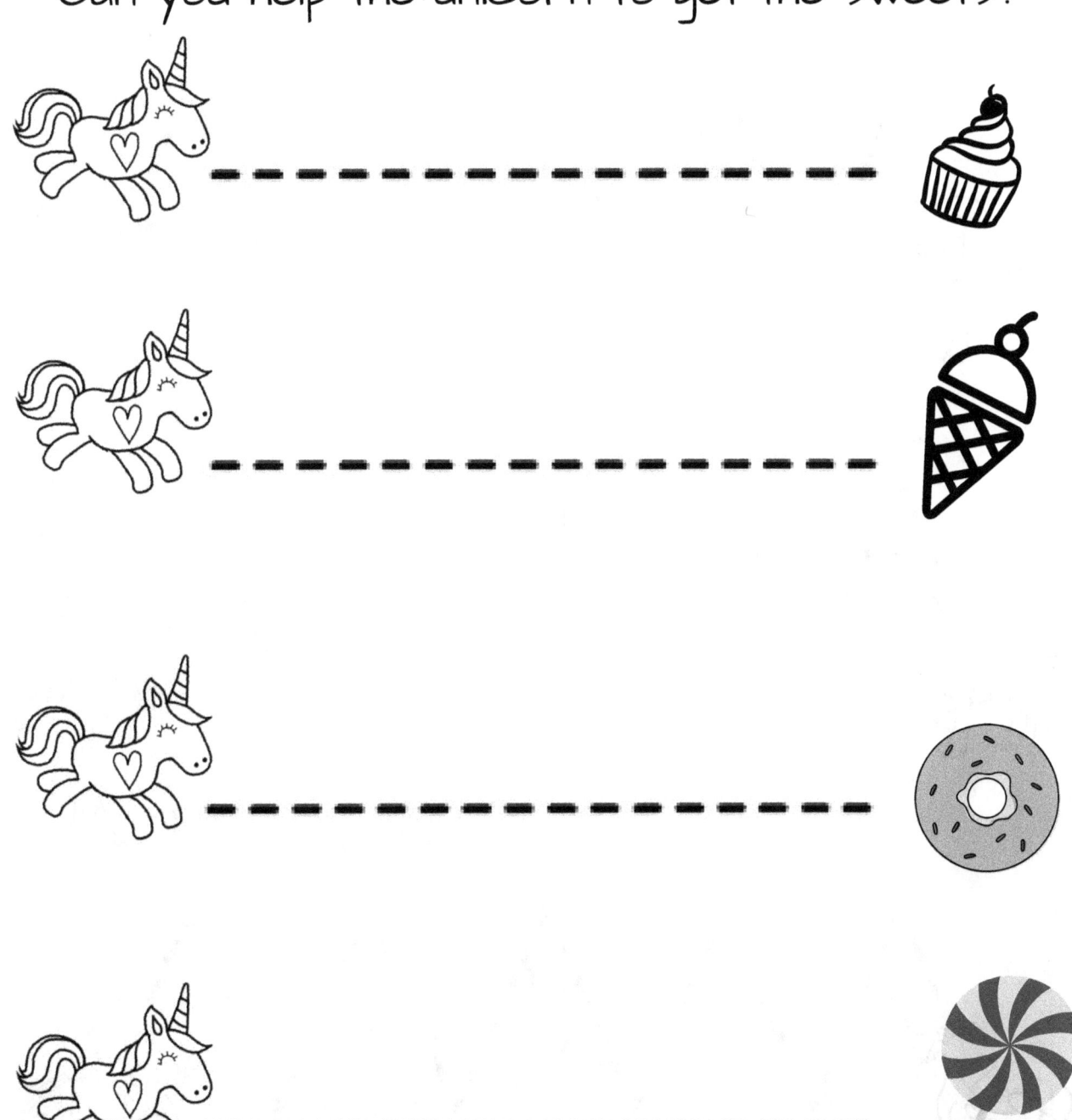

Writing Skill Game:

Can you help the unicorn to find the way to her friends?

Writing Skill Game:

Can you help the unicorn to find the way to the castle?

Writing Skill Game:

Can you help the baby unicorns tracing the lines to create shapes?

Writing Skill Game:

Can you guess the correct hidden letters?

U		I		O		N

S		A	R

	O	O	

C		O		D

R		I	B	W

Writing Skill Game:

Can you guess the correct hidden letters?

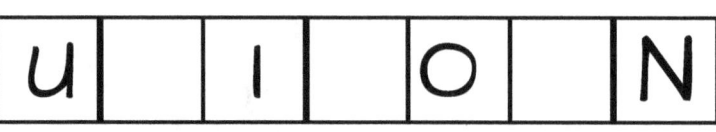

| U | | I | | O | | N |

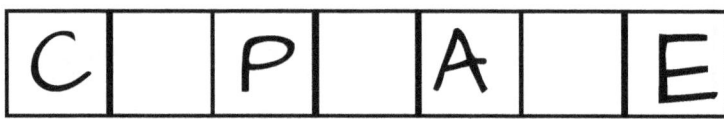

| C | | P | | A | | E |

| C | | | K | |

| D | | | N | | T |

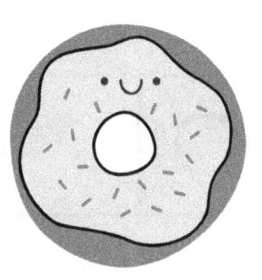

| I | | E | | R | | A |

Writing Skill Game:

Can you guess the correct hidden letters?

U		I		O		N

M		R		A		D

F		I		Y

D		A		O	

P		I		C		S	

Find and Color Game:

Which one is the unicorn?

Find and Color Game:
Can you color the unicorn with their assigned color?

1 - red   3 - yellow   5 - blue   7 - pink

2 - orange 4 - green   6 - violet 8 - white

Find and Color Game:
Where is the unicorn?

Find and Color Game:

Which one is the unicorn?

Find and Color Game:
Can you color the unicorn with their assigned color?

1 - violet   3 - yellow   5 - red

2 - pink   4 - orange   6 - blue

Find and Color Game:

Where are the 2 unicorns?

Find and Color Game:
Can you color the unicorn with their assigned color?

1 - pink   3 - yellow   5 - blue

2 - violet   4 - orange   6 - red

Find and Color Game:

Which one is the unicorn?

Find and Color Game:

Where are the 3 unicorns?

Maze Challenge:
Which path should the unicorn take way to her friends?

Maze Challenge:
Can you help the unicorn to get the ice cream?

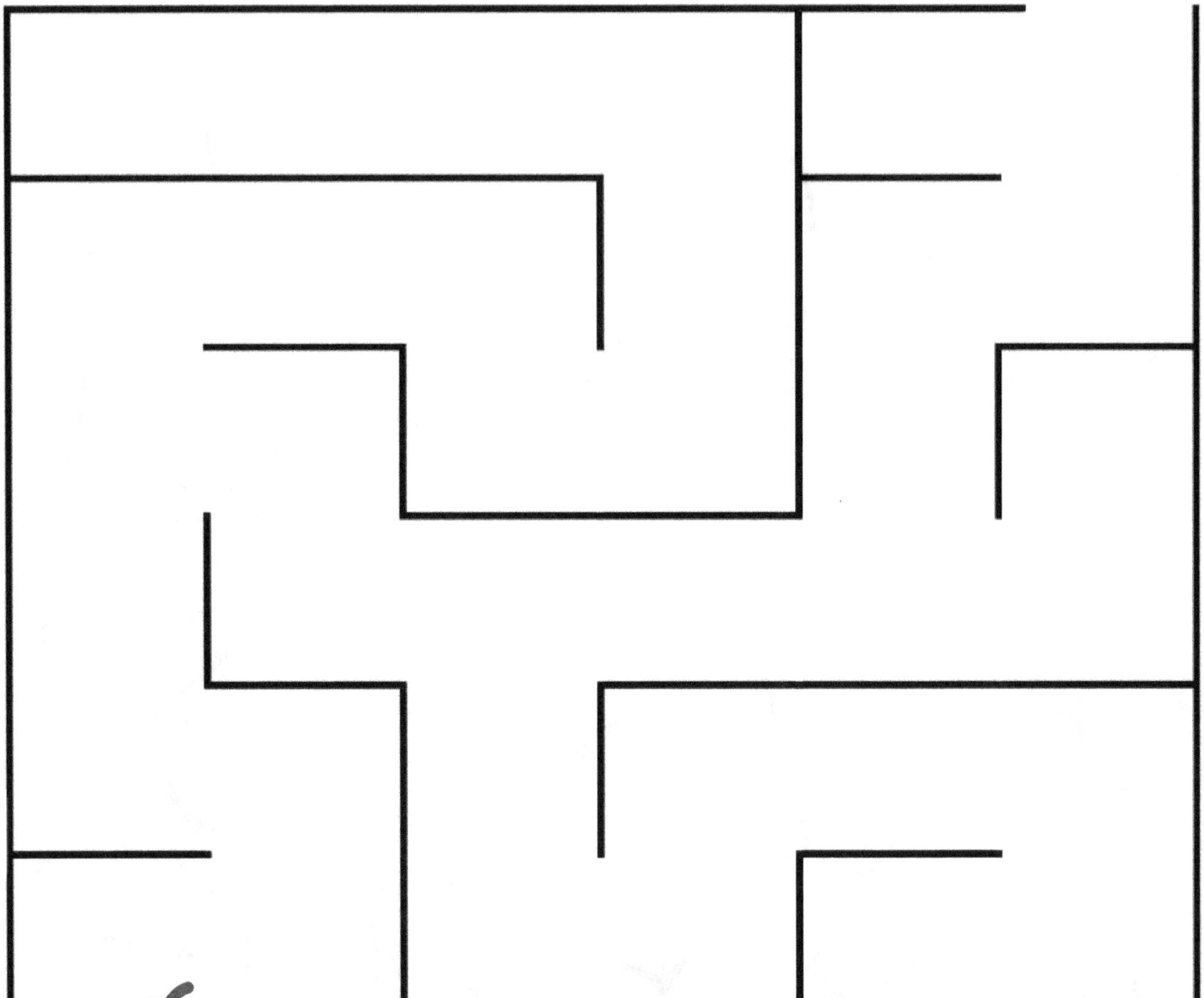

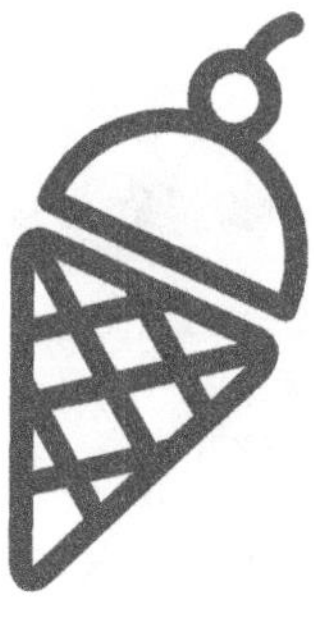

Maze Challenge:

Can you help the unicorn to get the cupcake?

Maze Challenge:

Can you help the unicorn
and the fairy to find
their way to the
magic land?

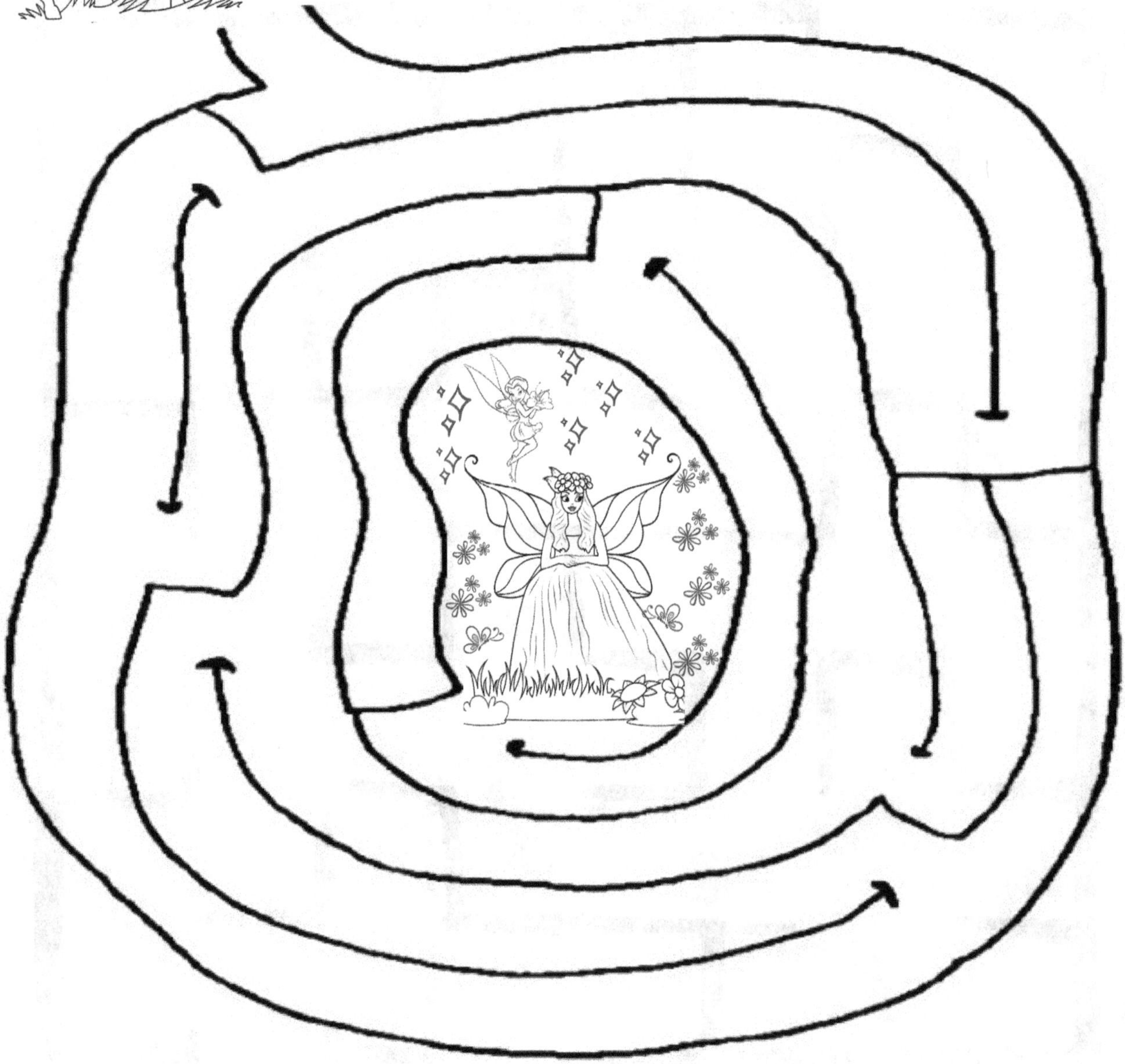

Maze Challenge: Can you help the flying unicorn and her friends to get the magic wand?

Maze Challenge:

Can you help the unicorn to get the cake?

Maze Challenge:
Can you guide the unicorn
to get the gift?

Maze Challenge: Can you help the the unicorn to find the way to the rainbow clouds?

Maze Challenge:

Can you help the unicorn to save the princess?

Dot to dots challenge:
Can you connect the dots to create a cute unicorn?

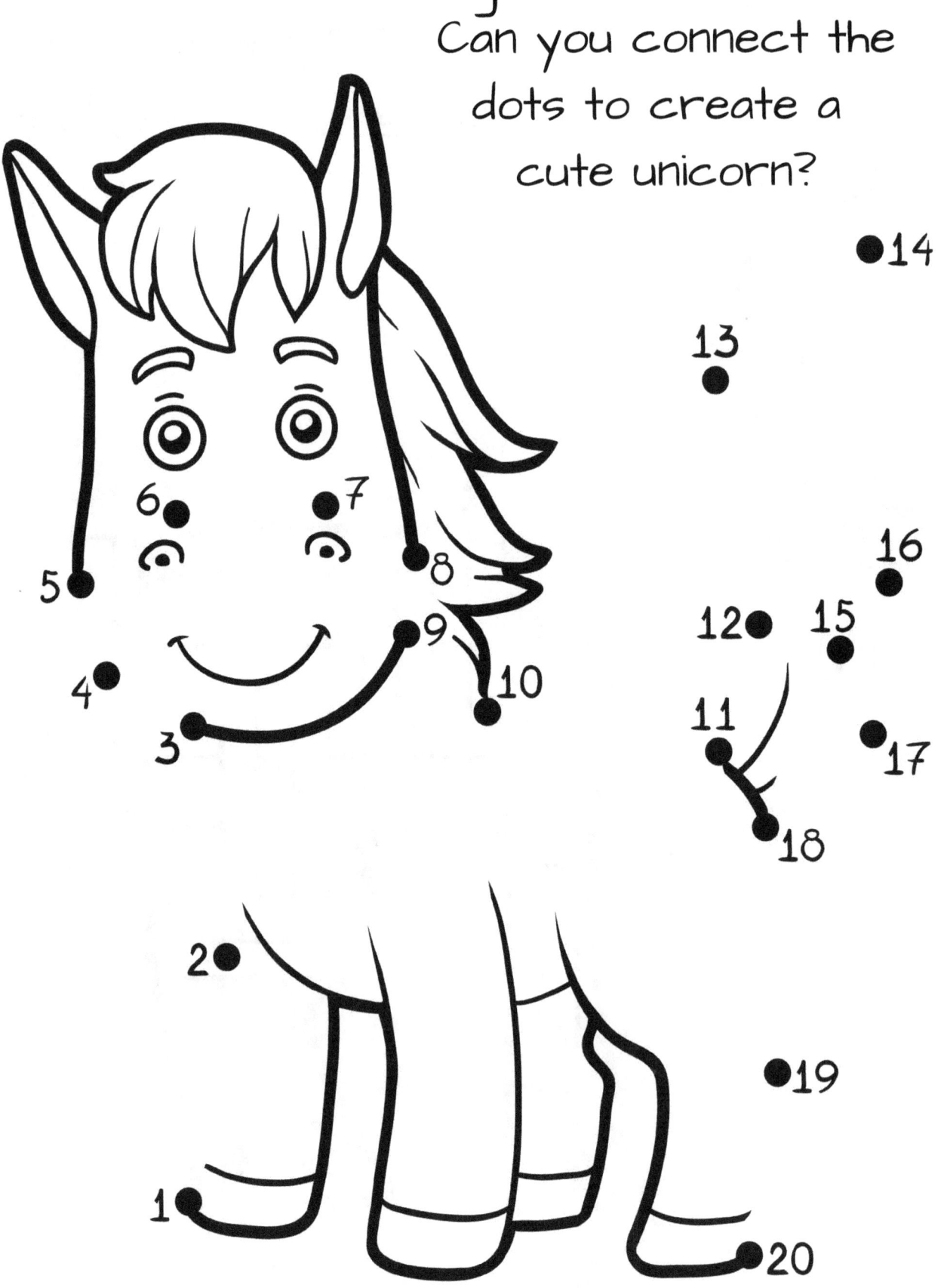

Dot to dots challenge:
Can you connect the dots to create
an adorable unicorn?

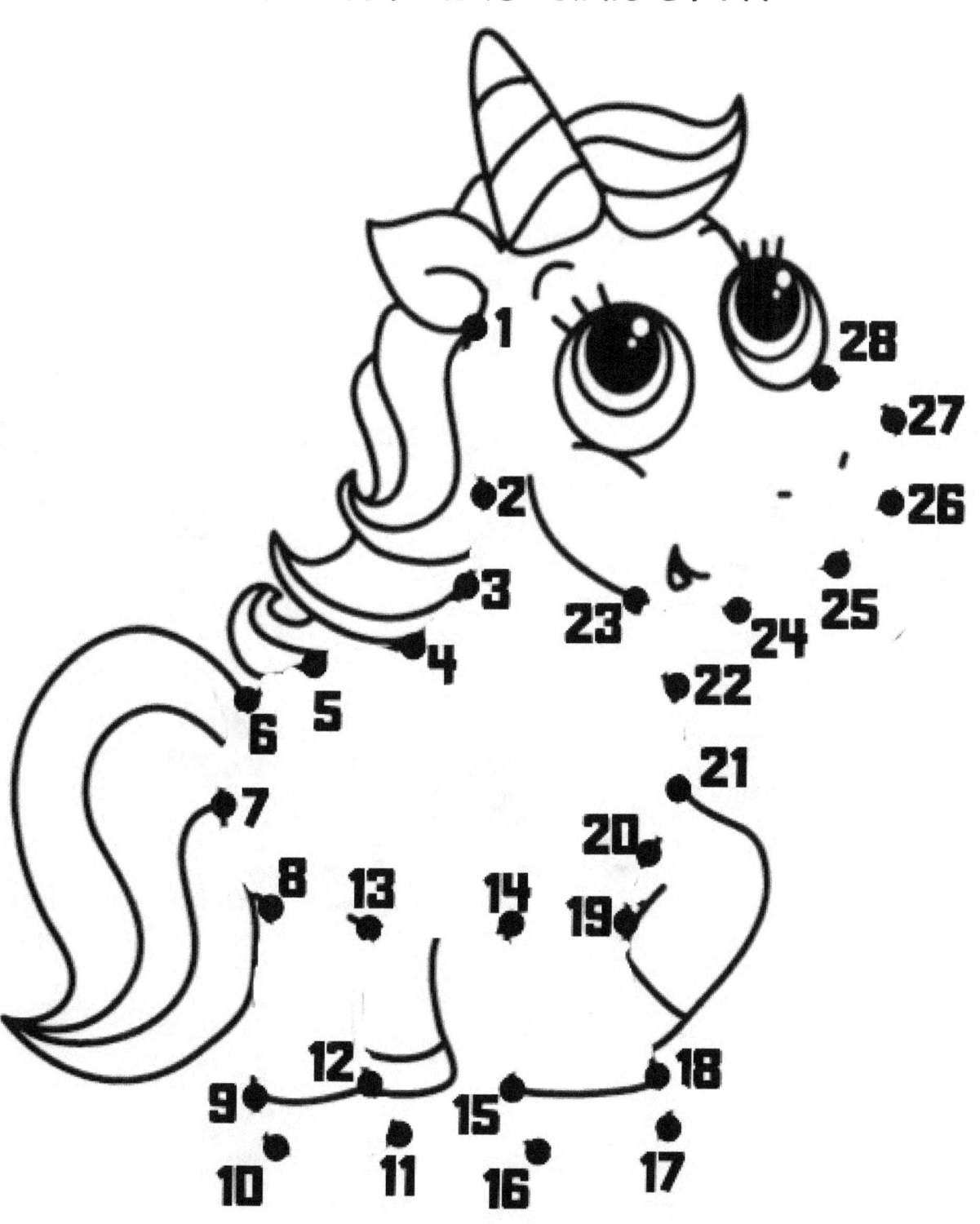

Dot to dots challenge:
Can you connect the dots to create a pretty unicorn?

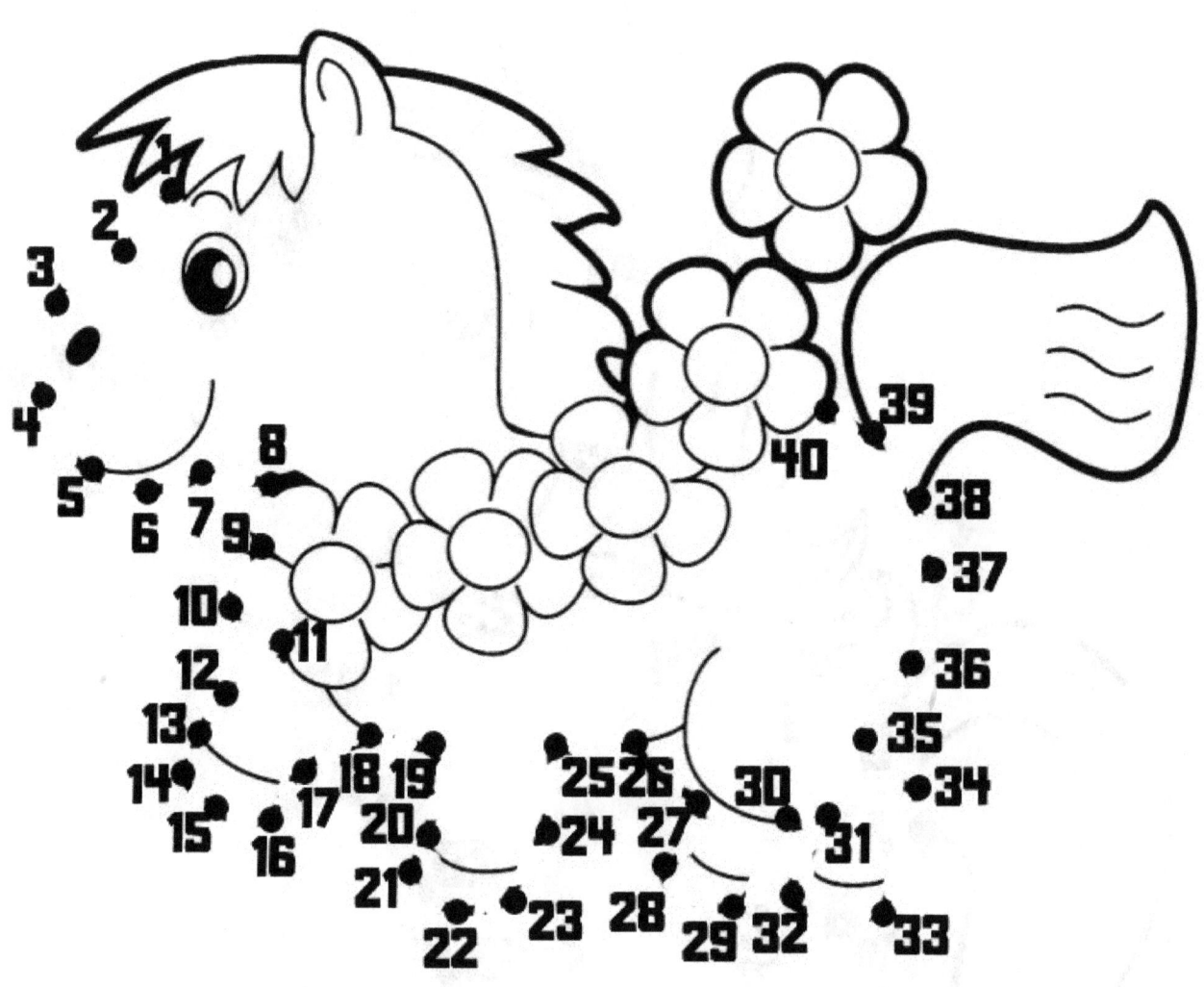

Dot to dots challenge:
Can you connect the dots to create
a flying unicorn?

Dot to dots challenge:

Can you connect the dots to create a lovely unicorn?

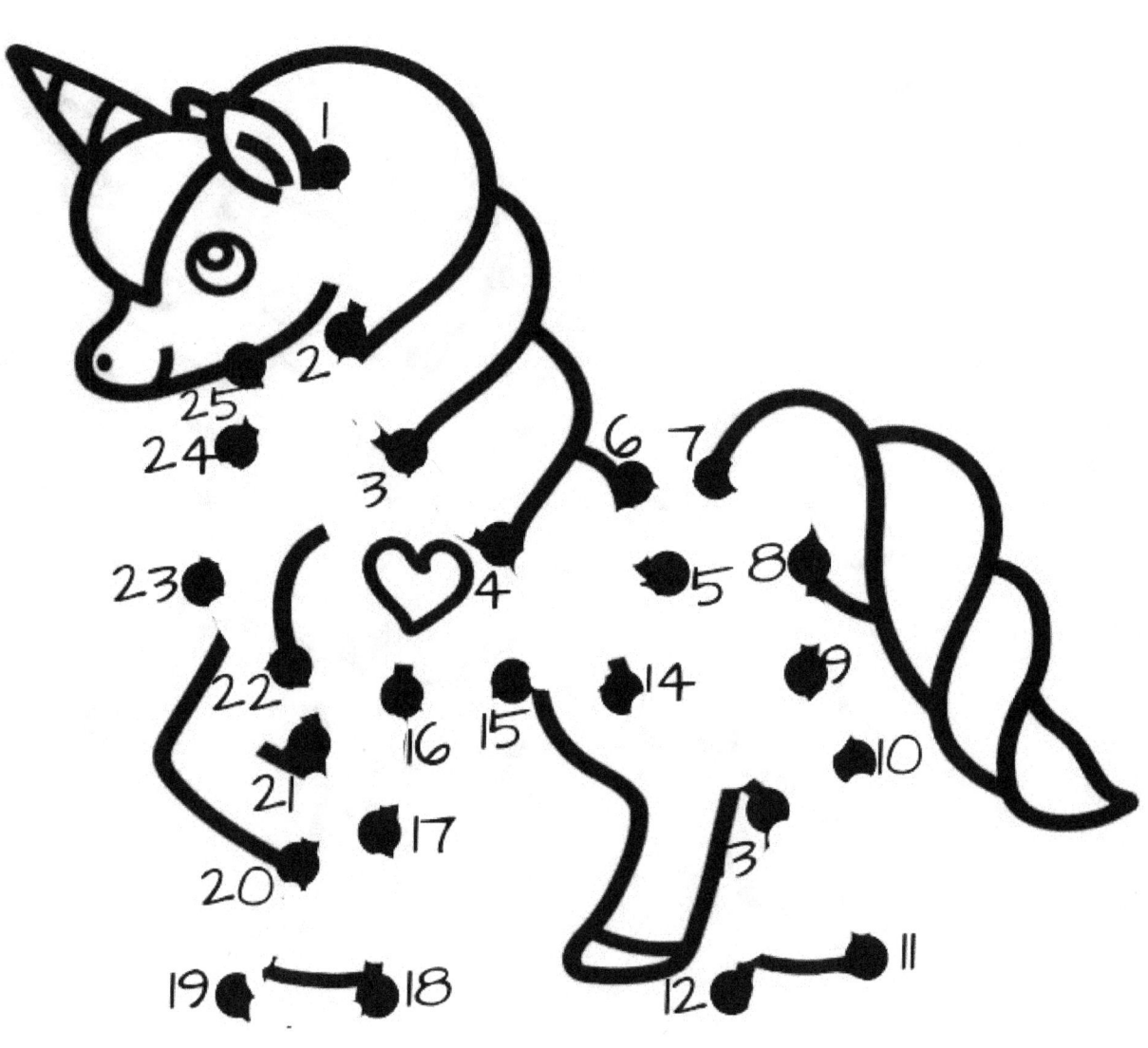

Dot to dots challenge:
Can you connect the dots to create a gorgeous unicorn?

Dot to dots challenge:
Can you connect
the dots to create
a magical unicorn?

32

33

31 30

34

29

28

27

23

24 26

25

22

21

35

20 19

10 18

11

36

8 9

17

13 12 16

15

37

14

7

38

6

39

5

4

3

2

1

Dot to dots challenge:

Can you connect the dots to create a fascinating unicorn?

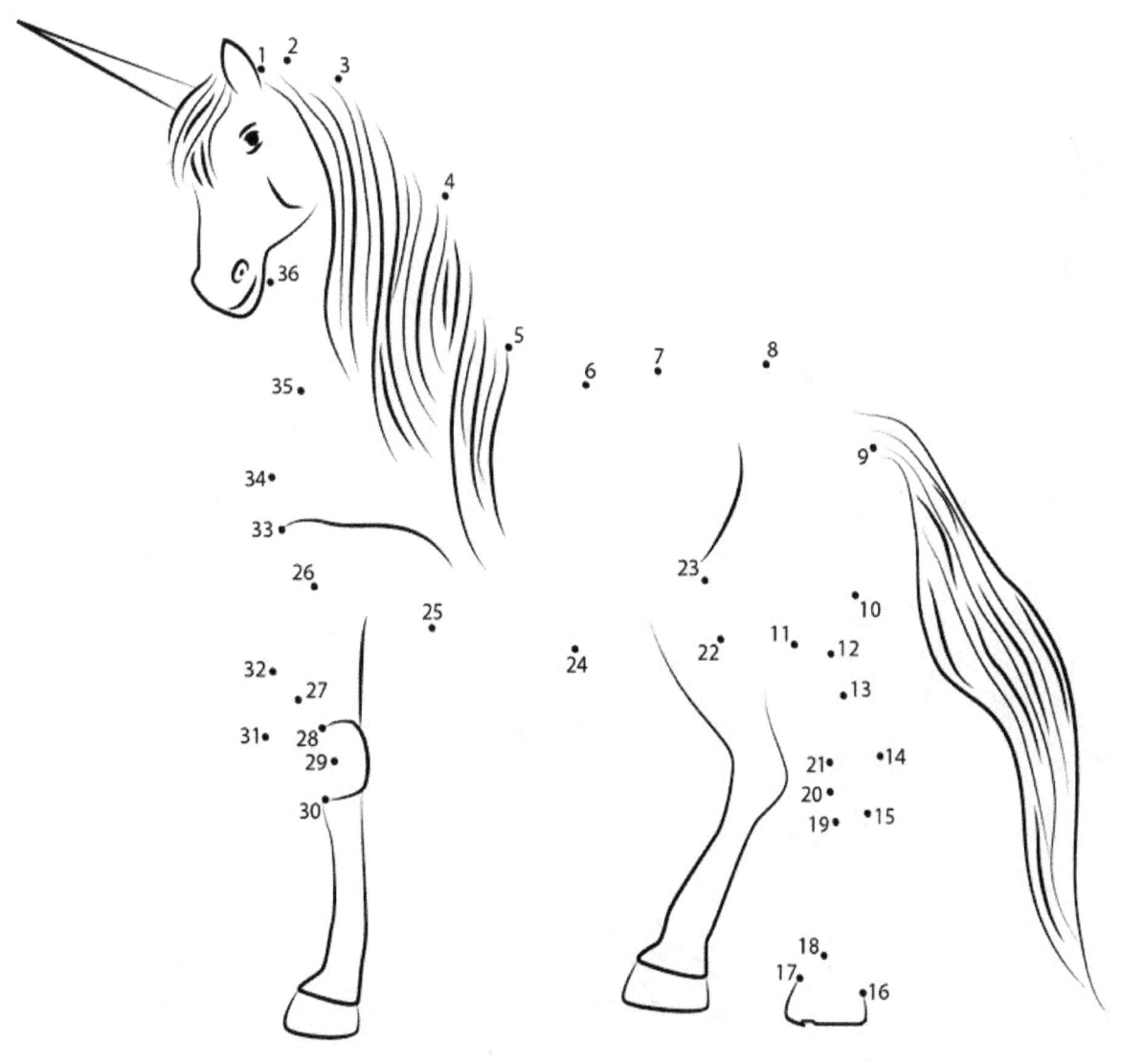

Dot to dots challenge:
Can you connect the dots to create a charming unicorn?

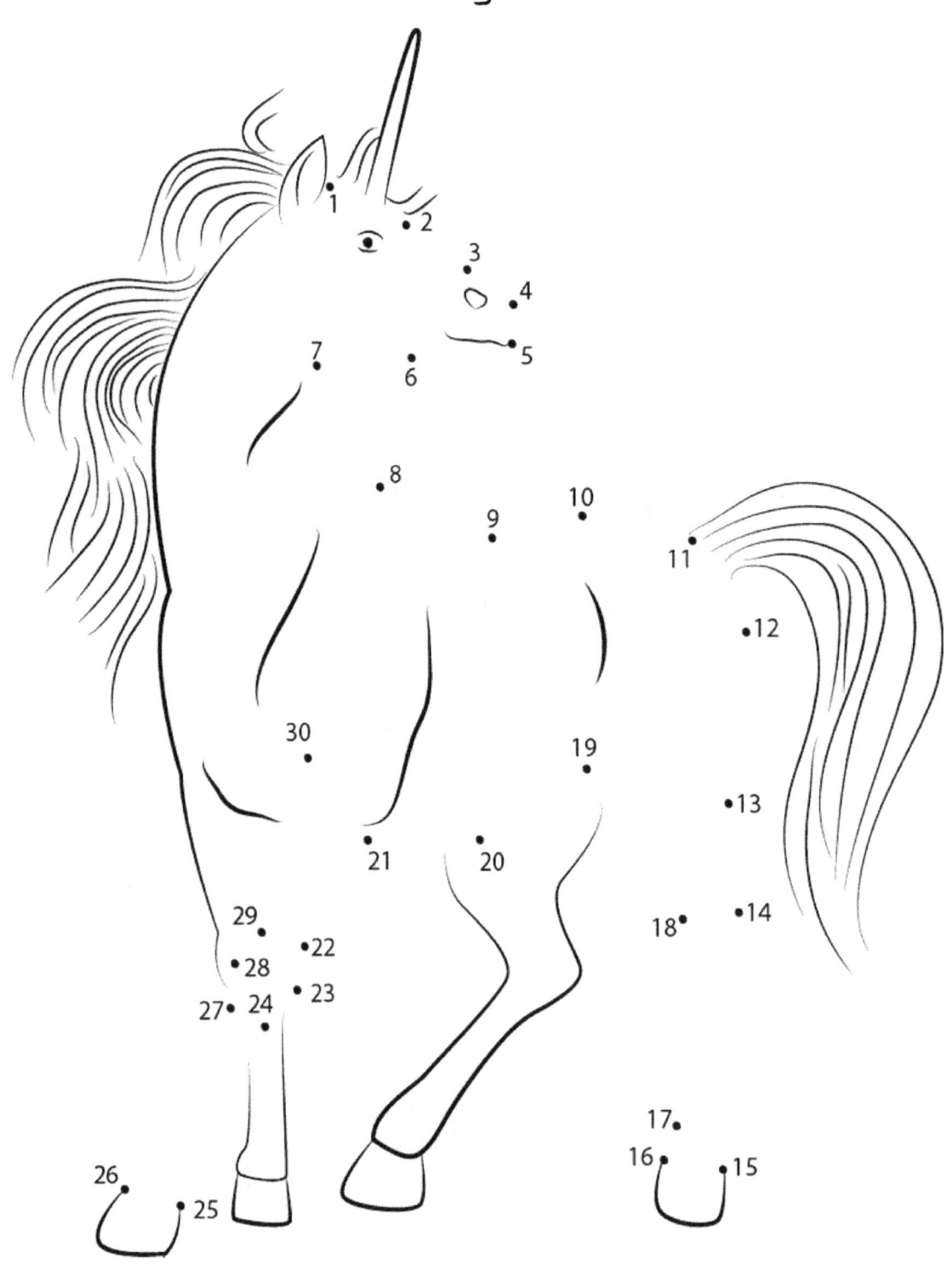

Matching Test:
Can you draw a line from each picture to the matching word?

moon

rainbow

unicorn

heart

star

Matching Test:
Can you draw a line to match the correct unicorn's shadow?

Matching Test:

Can you draw a line from each picture to the matching word?

cupcake

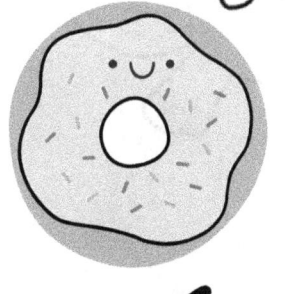

cake

unicorn

donut

ice cream

Matching Test:
Can you encircle which two baby unicorns are twins?

Matching Test:
Can you draw a line from each picture to the matching word?

dragon

unicorn

dinosaur

Matching Test:
Can you encircle the 3 matching unicorns ?

Let's party!

Matching Test:

Can you draw a line to match the unicorn parents to their children?

Matching Test:

Can you encircle the two unicorns
that are exactly the same?

Matching Test:

Can you draw a line from each picture to the matching word?

mermaid

princess

unicorn

fairy

Spot the Difference Game:
Which one is different from the others?

Spot the Difference Game:

Can you spot the
2 differences
between the
pictures?

Spot the Difference Game:

Which one is different from the others?

Spot the Difference Game:

Can you find and encircle the 3 differences between the pictures?

Spot the Difference Game:

Which one is different from the others?

Spot the Difference Game:

Can you spot the 4 differences ?

Spot the Difference Game:

Which one is different from the others?

Spot the Difference Game:

Can you encircle the 5 differences?

Spot the Difference Game:

Which one is different from the others?

Crossword Puzzle Game:
Can you guess the hidden letters?

S _ _ R _ C

U N _ C _ R

H _ _ R T

L

Crossword Puzzle Game:
Can you guess the hidden letters?

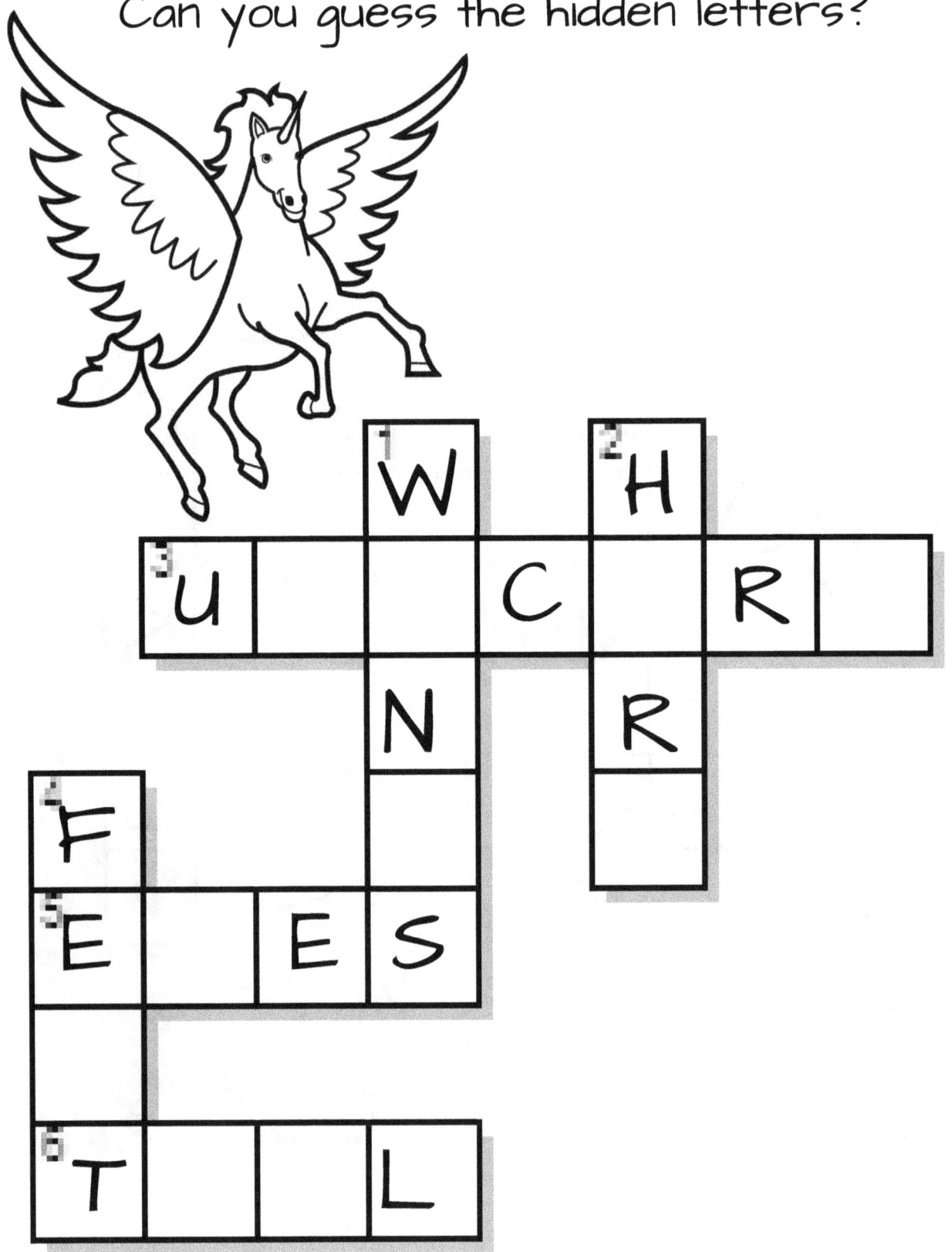

Crossword Puzzle Game:
Can you guess the hidden letters?

Crossword Puzzle Game:

Can you guess the
hidden letters?

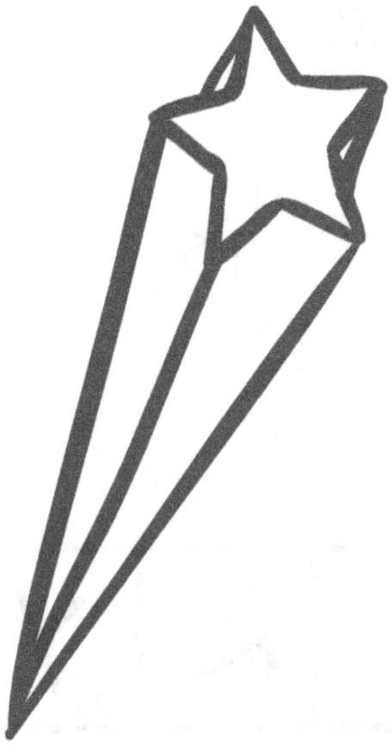

S

B U _ _ _ _ R _ _ Y

R

C

N

F _ _ W _

N

W

Crossword Puzzle Game:

Can you guess the hidden letters?

Crossword Puzzle Game:
Can you guess the hidden letters?

Crossword Puzzle Game:

Can you guess the hidden letters?

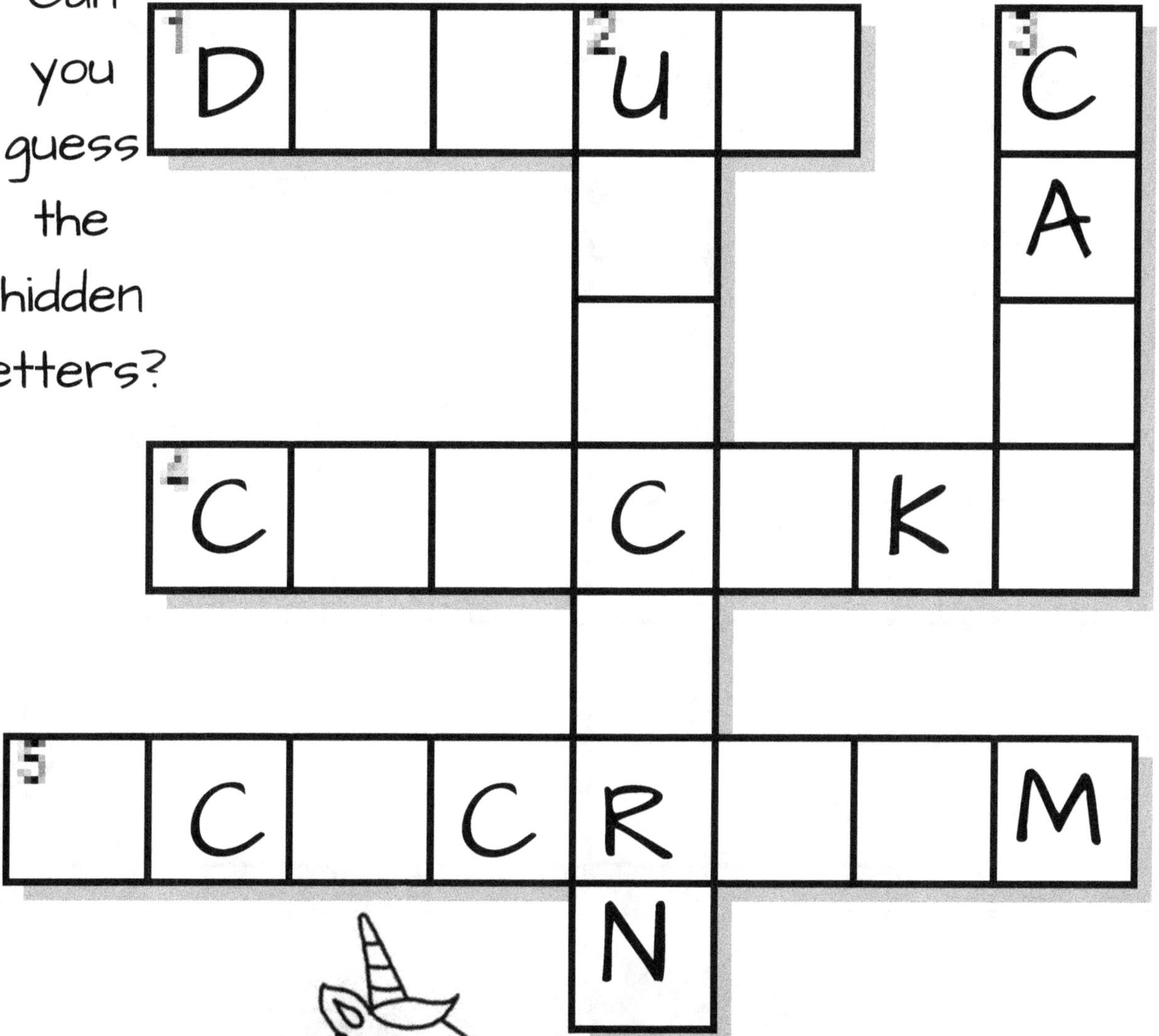

1 D
2 U
3 C
A
4 C
C
K
5
C
C
R
M
N

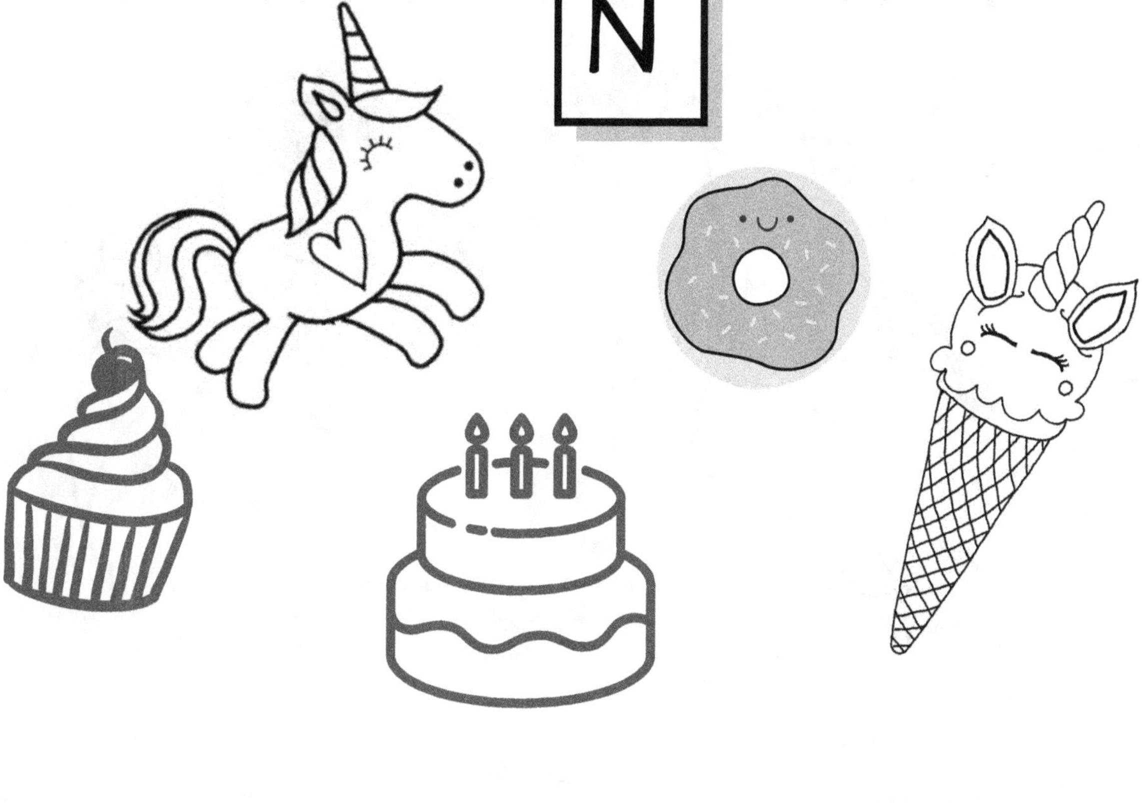

Crossword Puzzle Game:

Can you
guess the
hidden
letters?

1. U
2. D
3. D

Crossword Puzzle Game:

Can you guess the hidden letters?

Word Search Challenge:

Can you look for the 6 magical words?

F P W J K C A U P H
G F Q R S B Z N M X
W N X K T N K I O B
B C X X A G R C O D
Y L Z E R A G O N I
G O G N N E K R D V
D U U L W S U N T S
I D D S H L K Q C X
R A I N B O W D A W
C P H Z R G E R I S

UNICORN	CLOUD	RAINBOW
STAR	SUN	MOON

Word Search Challenge:

Can you search for the 6 words?

```
S  B  C  A  W  I  P  G  S  E
T  U  J  C  Y  X  D  G  H  K
F  T  U  V  F  G  R  M  D  I
A  T  N  O  L  G  A  A  K  E
I  E  I  A  O  N  G  G  B  P
R  R  C  N  W  M  O  I  C  N
Y  F  O  H  E  A  N  C  A  U
D  L  R  W  R  V  F  E  A  Z
W  Y  N  E  N  U  L  O  S  W
P  D  D  A  E  Z  Y  Y  N  R
```

UNICORN   FAIRY   BUTTERFLY
DRAGONFLY FLOWER   MAGIC

Word Search Challenge:

Can you find the 6 magical creature words?

```
G  A  K  F  T  Q  Y  U  T  J
D  Y  C  P  P  C  H  N  Y  Q
R  S  M  E  R  M  A  I  D  P
A  M  F  T  I  T  R  C  Y  Y
G  Y  A  H  N  Q  C  O  G  Z
O  X  I  R  C  T  A  R  Z  Q
N  J  R  E  E  N  S  N  P  P
V  R  Y  F  S  X  T  R  B  U
U  X  K  U  S  S  L  Q  E  I
W  R  Y  P  E  F  E  S  M  E
```
_____

| UNICORN | MERMAID | PRINCESS |
| FAIRY | CASTLE | DRAGON |

Word Search Challenge:

Can you look for the 7 animal words?

F P U N I C O R N R

S P L K E O J T F H

H J M L L X N U Z I

G U G P E L K R A N

V Y I B P I G I V O

W J R Z H O J N V C

B R A E A N W G W E

F Q F B N A Q I M R

L E F R T I G E R O

Q I E A Q R C K Z S

UNICORN   GIRAFFE   ZEBRA

ELEPHANT   RHINOCEROS LION

TIGER

Word Search Challenge:

Can you look for the 7 delicious words?

```
M H N W C I W S Q D
D C Z X M O Z D Q O
C A C I T R D D I N
U K Q I I U G Q N U
P E J C R E A M O T
C M P E A C U Y D L
A G Q S I G M S H S
K X D P I Z Z A B U
E Z G Y O C Y T X K
U N I C O R N Q N U
```

UNICORN   DONUT   ICE

CREAM   CAKE   PIZZA

CUPCAKE

Word Search Challenge:

Can you search for the unicorn's part of the body?

```
O  D  W  I  N  G  S  W  M  Q
J  J  J  E  O  L  O  A  O  S
O  Z  F  E  E  T  M  V  A  R
Y  Q  F  V  F  F  L  M  P  V
T  A  I  L  E  Y  E  S  C  H
G  T  M  N  N  N  K  H  E  F
V  H  O  S  G  E  U  O  F  R
N  J  U  N  I  C  O  R  N  P
V  S  T  P  Z  K  F  N  N  X
Q  I  H  X  W  E  S  N  U  Y
```

UNICORN	HORN	WINGS
TAIL	EYES	FEET
MOUTH	NECK	

Word Search Challenge:

Can you find the 7 different shapes?

```
D  N  W  S  X  N  P  H  N  R
Q  R  T  Q  V  N  L  Z  S  E
Z  A  P  U  S  X  K  S  Q  C
U  D  I  A  M  O  N  D  A  T
N  J  N  R  T  V  R  W  Z  A
I  R  T  E  E  H  Z  Y  G  N
C  I  R  C  L  E  B  U  Z  G
O  B  D  A  R  A  M  S  Q  L
R  S  S  T  A  R  Q  Z  I  E
N  J  Z  G  R  T  P  B  X  C
```

UNICORN   STAR   HEART
CIRCLE   SQUARE   DIAMOND
RECTANGLE

Word Search Challenge:

Can you search for the
5 magical creatures?

P B F A I R Y Z E N

E S D B Y R Y L S O

S U X C I K T U O G

O S S J L S J Q C A

H S E V A U I X B R

U N I C O R N U F D

A Z X F N W R W R G

X I X R I I I G S B

L I G F Z T R W Z J

Y N N F L G L P P X

UNICORN   PRINCESS   FAIRY

DRAGON   CASTLE

Word Search Challenge:

Can you search for the 6 creatures?

Y D R A G O N F L Y

J M E R M A I D X U

Z H U M R G F D Y V

T C G E F Q E C P Q

N F K Z R P Y Y B L

M V B K F V Z C U D

R U A S O N I D J R

U N I C O R N K H E

S O R E C O N I H R

Q P E G A S U S P G

UNICORN   DINOSAUR   DRAGONFLY

RHINOCEROS MERMAID   PEGASUS

Counting Skills Challenge:

How many unicorns are there?

Counting Skills Challenge:

Can you count how many baby unicorns are there?

Counting Skills Challenge:

How many unicorns are there?

Counting Skills Challenge:

Can you color the star of the correct count?

Counting Skills Challenge:

Can you color the cloud of the correct count?

Counting Skills Challenge:

Can you draw a line to the star of the correct corresponding count?

Counting Skills Challenge:
Can you draw a line to the cloud of the correct corresponding count?

Counting Skills Challenge:

Can you write inside the star the correct count
of the flying baby unicorns?

Counting Skills Challenge:

Can you write inside the cloud the correct count of the flying unicorns?

Answers

Writing Skill Game:

Uu is for *Unicorn*

U U U U U U

u u u u u u

Find and Color Game:

Can you color the unicorn with their assigned color?

1 - pink   3 - red   5 - yellow

2 - violet   4 - orange   6 - blue

Maze Challenge:

Can you help the unicorn to find the way to the castle?

castle

Dot to dots challenge:

Can you connect the dots to create a charming unicorn?

Matching Test:

Can you encircle the correct unicorn's shadow?

Spot the Difference Game:

Can you find and encircle the difference?

Crossword Puzzle Game:

Can you guess the hidden letters?

MOON
STAR
RAINBOW
UNICORN
CLOUD

Word Search Challenge:

Can you find the 5 unicorn words?

UNICORN   UNICORN   UNICORN
UNICORN   UNICORN

Counting Skills Challenge:

Can you count how many unicorns?

3

Answers for Writing Skill Games

Writing Skill Game: Can you draw the capital letter U?

Writing Skill Game: Can you draw the small letter u?

Writing Skill Game:

Can you help the unicorn to get the sweets?

Writing Skill Game:

Can you help the unicorn to find the way to her friends?

Writing Skill Game:

Can you help the unicorn to find the way to the castle?

Writing Skill Game:

Can you help the baby unicorns tracing the lines to create shapes?

Writing Skill Game:

Can you guess the correct hidden letters?

UNICORN
STAR
MOON
CLOUD
RAINBOW

Writing Skill Game:

Can you guess the correct hidden letters?

UNICORN
CUPCAKE
CAKE
DONUT
ICECREAM

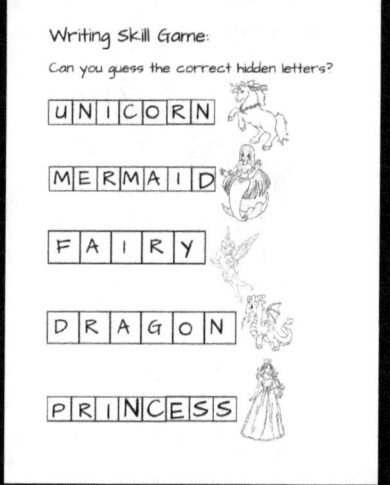

Writing Skill Game:

Can you guess the correct hidden letters?

UNICORN
MERMAID
FAIRY
DRAGON
PRINCESS

Answers for Find and Color Games

Find and Color Game:

Which one is the unicorn?

Find and Color Game:
Can you color the unicorn with their assigned color?

1 - red   3 - yellow   5 - blue   7 - pink

2 - orange 4 - green   6 - violet 8 - white

Find and Color Game:

Where is the unicorn?

Find and Color Game:

Which one is the unicorn?

Find and Color Game:
Can you color the unicorn with their assigned color?

1 - violet   3 - yellow   5 - red

2 - pink   4 - orange   6 - blue

Find and Color Game:

Where are the 2 unicorns?

Find and Color Game:
Can you color the unicorn with their assigned color?

1 - pink   3 - yellow   5 - blue

2 - violet   4 - orange   6 - red

Find and Color Game:

Which one is the unicorn?

Find and Color Game:

Where are the 3 unicorns?

Answers for Mazes Challenges

Maze Challenge:
Which path should the unicorn take way to her friends?

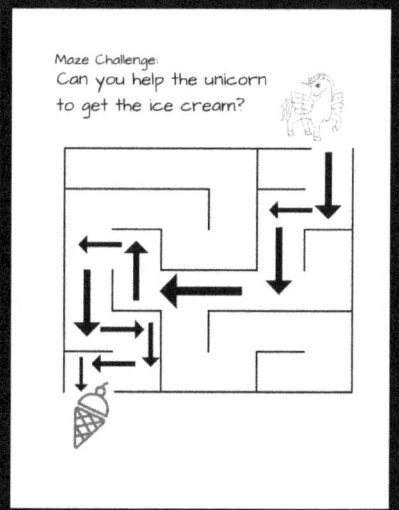

Maze Challenge:
Can you help the unicorn to get the ice cream?

Maze Challenge:
Can you help the unicorn to get the cupcake?

Maze Challenge:
Can you help the unicorn and the fairy to find their way to the magic land?

Maze Challenge: Can you help the flying unicorn and her friends to get the magic wand?

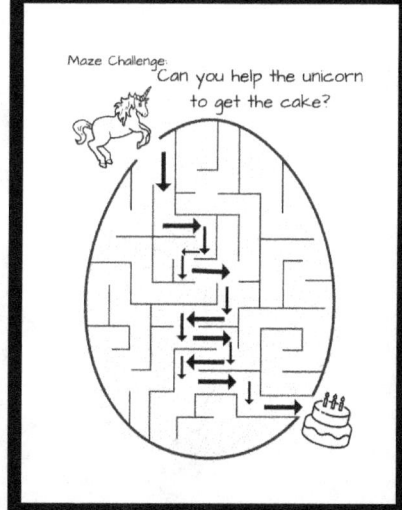

Maze Challenge:
Can you help the unicorn to get the cake?

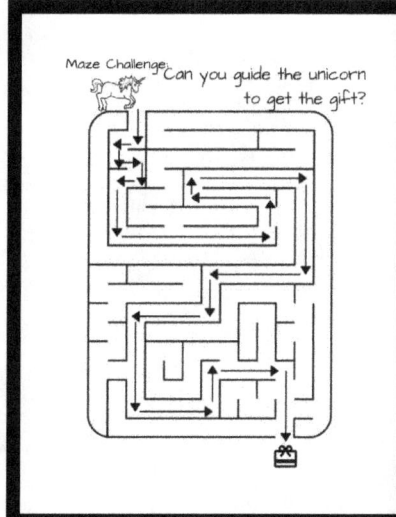

Maze Challenge: Can you guide the unicorn to get the gift?

Maze Challenge: Can you help the the unicorn to find the way to the rainbow clouds?

Maze Challenge:
Can you help the unicorn to save the princess?

Answers for Dot to Dot Challenges

Dot to dots challenge:
Can you connect the dots to create a cute unicorn?

Dot to dots challenge:
Can you connect the dots to create an adorable unicorn?

Dot to dots challenge:
Can you connect the dots to create a pretty unicorn?

Dot to dots challenge:
Can you connect the dots to create a flying unicorn?

Dot to dots challenge:
Can you connect the dots to create a fascinating unicorn?

Dot to dots challenge:
Can you connect the dots to create a gorgeous unicorn?

Dot to dots challenge:
Can you connect the dots to create a magical unicorn?

Dot to dots challenge:
Can you connect the dots to create a lovely unicorn?

Dot to dots challenge:
Can you connect the dots to create a charming unicorn?

Answers for Matching Games

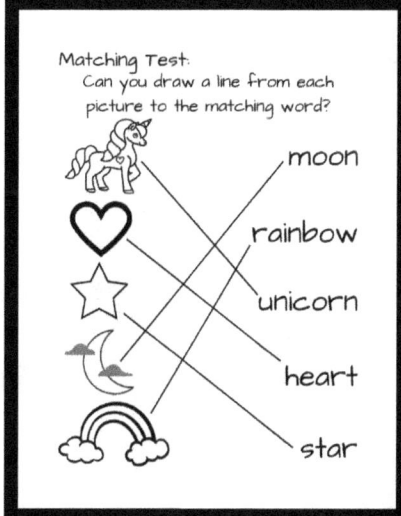

Matching Test:
Can you draw a line from each picture to the matching word?

moon

rainbow

unicorn

heart

star

Matching Test:
Can you draw a line to match the correct unicorn's shadow?

Matching Test:
Can you draw a line from each picture to the matching word?

cupcake

cake

unicorn

donut

ice cream

Matching Test:
Can you encircle which two baby unicorns are twins?

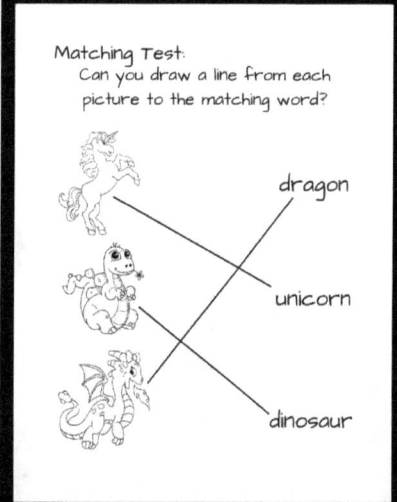

Matching Test:
Can you draw a line from each picture to the matching word?

dragon

unicorn

dinosaur

Matching Test:
Can you encircle the 3 matching unicorns ?

Let's party!

Matching Test:
Can you draw a line to match the unicorn parents to their children?

Matching Test:
Can you encircle the two unicorns that are exactly the same?

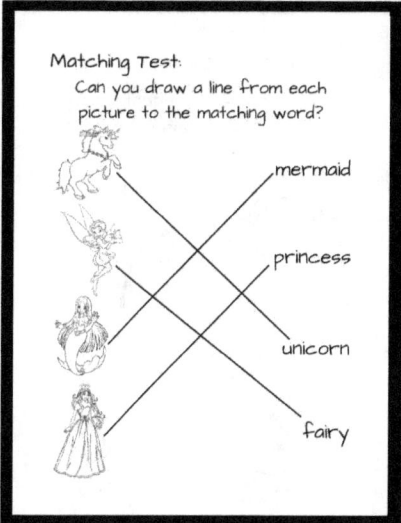

Matching Test:
Can you draw a line from each picture to the matching word?

mermaid

princess

unicorn

fairy

Answers for Spot the Difference GAmes

Answers for Crossword Puzzle

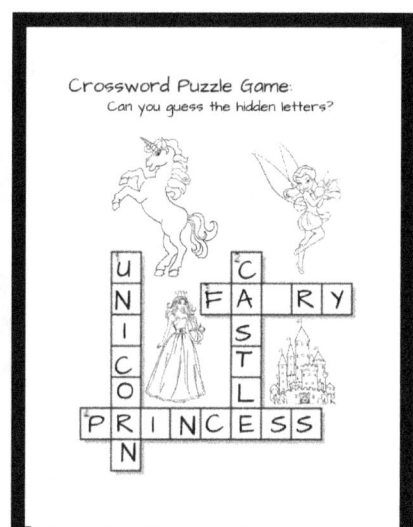

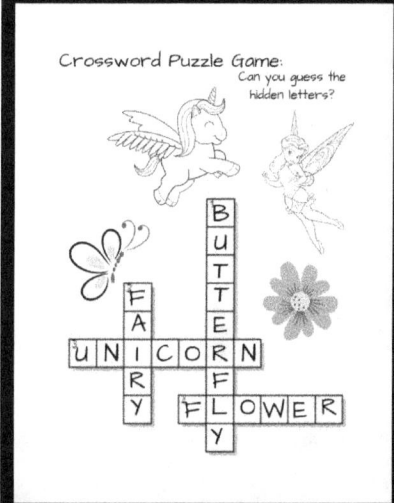

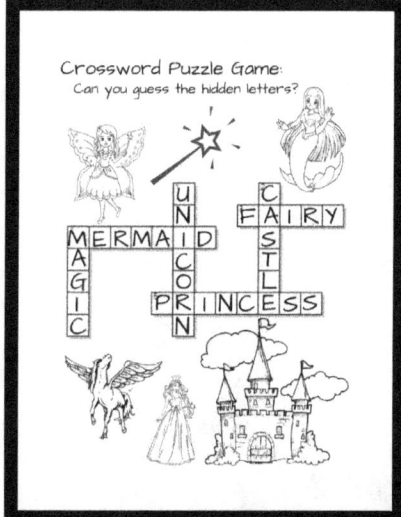

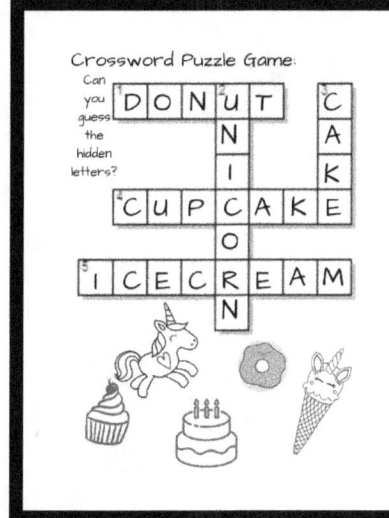

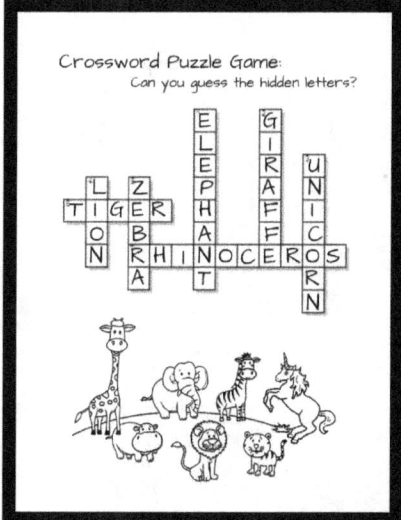

Answers for Word Search Games

Word Search Challenge:
Can you look for the 6 magical words?

```
F P W J K C A U P H
G F Q R S B Z N M X
W N X K T N K I O B
B C X X A G R C O D
Y L Z E R A G O N V
G O G N N E K R D V
D U U L W S U N T S
I D D S H L K Q C X
R A I N B O W D A W
C P H Z R G E R I S
```

UNICORN CLOUD RAINBOW
STAR SUN MOON

Word Search Challenge:
Can you search for the 6 words?

```
S B C A W I P G S E
T U J C Y X D G H K
F T U V F G R M D I
A E N O L G A A K E
I R I A O N G G B P
R C N W M O I C N
Y F O H E A N C A U
D L R W R V F E A Z
W Y N E N U L O S W
P D D A E Z Y Y N R
```

UNICORN FAIRY BUTTERFLY
DRAGONFLY FLOWER MAGIC

Word Search Challenge:
Can you find the 6 magical creature words?

```
G A K F T Q Y U T J
D Y C P P C H N Y Q
R S M E R M A I D P
A M F T I T R C Y Y
G Y A H N Q C O G Z
O X I R C T A R Z Q
N J R E E N S N P P
V R Y F S X T R B U
U X K U S S L Q E I
W R Y P E F E S M E
```

UNICORN MERMAID PRINCESS
FAIRY CASTLE DRAGON

Word Search Challenge:
Can you look for the 7 animal words?

```
F P U N I C O R N R
S P L K E O J T F H
H J M L L X N U Z I
G U G P E L K R A N
V Y I B P I G I V O
W J R Z H O J N V C
B R A E A N W G W E
F Q F B N A Q I M R
L E F R T I G E R O
Q I E A Q R C K Z S
```

UNICORN GIRAFFE ZEBRA
ELEPHANT RHINOCEROS LION
TIGER

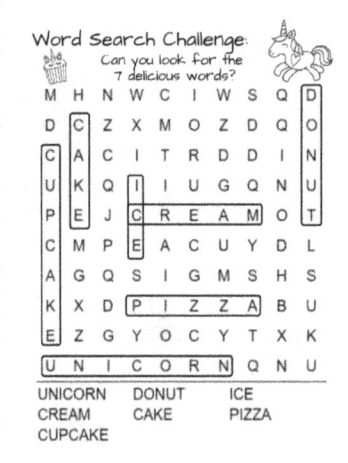

Word Search Challenge:
Can you look for the 7 delicious words?

```
M H N W C I W S Q D
D C Z X M O Z D Q O
C A C I T R D D I N
U K Q I I U G Q N U
P E J C R E A M O T
C M P E A C U Y D L
A G Q S I G M S H S
K X D P I Z Z A B U
E Z G Y O C Y T X K
U N I C O R N Q N U
```

UNICORN DONUT ICE
CREAM CAKE PIZZA
CUPCAKE

Word Search Challenge:
Can you search for the unicorn's part of the body?

```
O D W I N G S W M Q
J J J E O L O A O S
O Z F E E T M V A R
Y Q F V F F L M P V
T A I L E Y E S C H
G T M N N N K H E F
V H O S G E U O F R
N J U N I C O R N X
V S T P Z K F N N X
Q I H X W E S N U Y
```

UNICORN HORN WINGS
TAIL EYES FEET
MOUTH NECK

Word Search Challenge:
Can you find the 7 different shapes?

```
D N W S X N P H N R
Q R T Q V N L Z S E
Z A P U S X K S Q C
U D I A M O N D A T
N J N R T V R W Z A
I R T E E H Z Y G N
C I R C L E B U Z G
O B D A R A M S Q L
R S S T A R Q Z I E
N J Z G R T P B X C
```

UNICORN STAR HEART
CIRCLE SQUARE DIAMOND
RECTANGLE

Word Search Challenge:
Can you search for the 5 magical creatures?

```
P B F A I R Y Z E N
E S D B Y R Y L S O
S U X C I K T U O G
O S S J L S J Q C A
H S E V A U I X B R
U N I C O R N U F D
A Z X F N W R W R G
X I X R I I G S B
L I G F Z T R W Z J
Y N N F L G L P P X
```

UNICORN PRINCESS FAIRY
DRAGON CASTLE

Word Search Challenge:
Can you search for the 6 creatures?

```
Y D R A G O N F L Y
J M E R M A I D X U
Z H U M R G F D Y V
T C G E F Q E C P Q
N F K Z R P Y Y B L
M V B K F V Z C U D
R U A S O N I D J R
U N I C O R N K H E
S O R E C O N I H R
Q P E G A S U S P G
```

UNICORN DINOSAUR DRAGONFLY
RHINOCEROS MERMAID PEGASUS

Answers for Counting Skill Challenges

Counting Skills Challenge:
How many unicorns are there?

4

Counting Skills Challenge:
Can you count how many baby unicorns are there?

2

3

4

Counting Skills Challenge:
How many unicorns are there?

3

4

5

Counting Skills Challenge:
Can you color the star of the correct count?

1

2

3

Counting Skills Challenge:
Can you color the cloud of the correct count?

3

4

5

Counting Skills Challenge:
Can you draw a line to the star of the correct corresponding count?

5

3

4

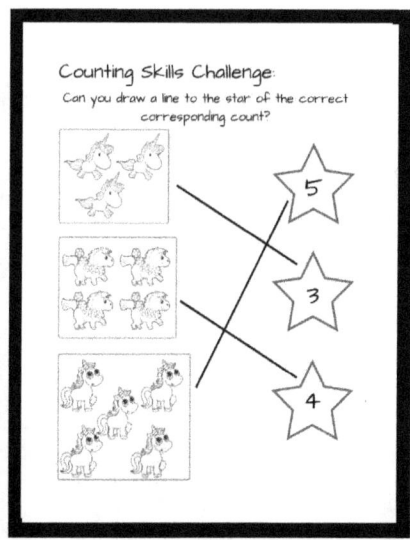

Counting Skills Challenge:
Can you draw a line to the cloud of the correct corresponding count?

6

4

8

10

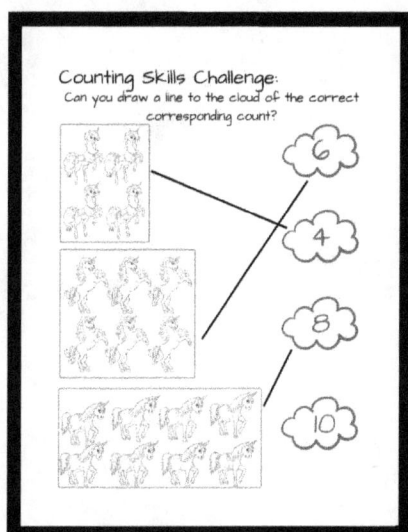

Counting Skills Challenge:
Can you write inside the star the correct count of the flying baby unicorns?

3

5

7

9

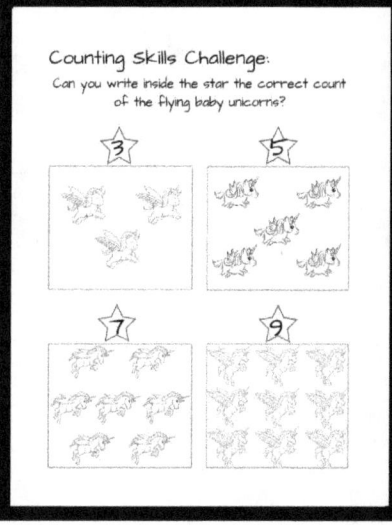

Counting Skills Challenge:
Can you write inside the cloud the correct count of the flying unicorns?

4

6

8

9

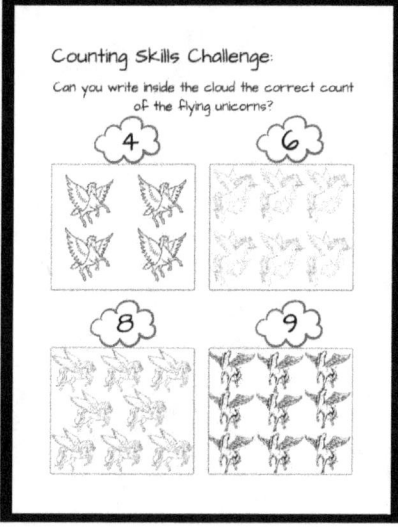

www.ingramcontent.com/pod-product-compliance
Lightning Source LLC
Chambersburg PA
CBHW080557060326
40689CB00021B/4890